ALASKA

TERRY DUNNAHOO

Franklin Watts
New York/London/Toronto/Sydney/1987
A First Book

Cover photographs courtesy of Alaska Division of Tourism

Photographs courtesy of Alaska Division of Tourism: pp. 11
(Yukon Visitors Bureau), 29, 37 (Bruce McAllister), 43, 47
(Mark Skok), 50 (Ben Davidson), 63 (top); Alaska Historical
Library: pp. 15 (Alaska Purchase Centennial Collection), 18
and 27 (bottom) (Skinner Collection), 27 (top) (A. G. Simmer);
The Alyeska Pipeline Service Company: p. 23; Will Yurman:
p. 33; Sitmar Cruises: p. 56; Alaska Department of Fish and
Game: p. 61; Alaska State Troopers: p. 63 (bottom).

Library of Congress Cataloging-in-Publication Data

Dunnahoo, Terry.
Alaska.

(A First book)
Includes index.
Summary: Discusses Alaska's history, its different
regions and cities, resources, wildlife, economy, and
daily life.
1. Alaska—Juvenile literature. [1. Alaska] I. Title.
F904.3.D84   1987   979.8   87-6277
ISBN 0-531-10375-7

TO ANNE WITH LOVE

CONTENTS

ALASKA

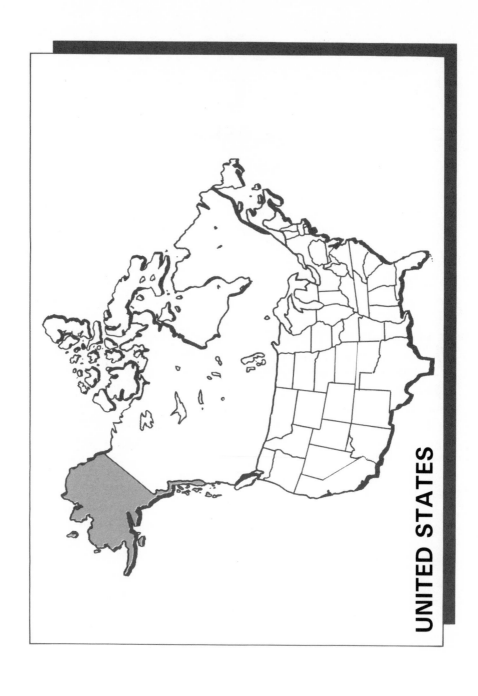

UNITED STATES

1

COMRADES TO CONSTITUTION

Many Alaskans claim that in the 1890s, a man survived a winter night by sleeping inside the carcass of a moose. In the morning, the carcass was frozen shut and he couldn't get out. He thought he would die there but wolves gnawed on the carcass and freed him. As with many tales Alaskans tell, this one may have started while people were entertaining themselves through a boring sub-zero night.

During the winter of 1917–18, to relieve boredom, the residents of Nenana began the Nenana Ice Classic. City officials today continue the tradition by rigging a tripod in the frozen Tanana River and connecting the tripod by wire to the clock in a tower on shore. As the ice breaks and begins its journey downstream, the tripod falls, the wire snaps and stops the clock. The person who comes closest to predicting the exact minute, hour, and day that this happens wins thousands of dollars. The breakup is considered the beginning of spring. The earliest the ice has broken is April 20, 1940. The latest date—May 20—was in 1964.

People talk often about winters in Alaska. And although winters are harsh in our forty-ninth state, they are warmer now than they were thousands of years ago. At that time, most of Alaska was buried under sheets of ice. This ice was not like the ice you skate on or the ice that forms on your sidewalk after a winter rain. This ice was thousands of feet thick and had covered a large area of the earth for millions of years. By the time the Ice Age—which is also known as the Pleistocene Epoch—ended 10,000 to 15,000 years ago, the melting had left mountains, glaciers, and lakes and was responsible for the shape of Alaska as we know it today.

During this time, Alaska and the Soviet Union were still connected by a 1,000-mile (1,600-km) land and ice bridge. The bridge was formed when Ice Age glaciers trapped so much moisture that oceans dropped 300 feet (90 m) below their present levels. Animals and people crossed the bridge in search of food and shelter. Anthropologists believe the first inhabitants of Alaska came across the Bering Strait from Asia before the melting ice raised sea levels and separated the continents.

RUSSIAN DISCOVERY

In the summer of 1741, Vitus Bering, a Danish explorer working for the Russian Navy, and Alexei Chirikov, a Russian naval officer under Bering's command, sighted Alaska. The name of Bering's ship was the *St. Peter.* Chirikov's ship was called the *St. Paul.* These men had made several trips together and had returned to Russia safely. On this trip, the ships became separated during a storm. Their commanders never saw each other again.

According to logs from the *St. Paul,* Chirikov saw land on July 15 near the southern coast of Alaska. He sailed northeast and three days later sent a boat crew ashore to explore. They did not return. He tried two more times. None of the men returned. Because he had no more boats to send, Chirikov headed back to Russia. He never learned what happened to his men. But a legend of the Tlingit Indians in southeastern Alaska tells of white men who long ago were ambushed by warriors dressed in bearskins.

Bering sighted land on July 16. When scouting parties went ashore, they saw no one and found little food. By September, the crew was exhausted and weak. After Captain Bering and many of the men became ill, they started for Russia. But the ship was wrecked

—10

*The Lowell Glacier, one of many
glaciers that exist in Alaska today*

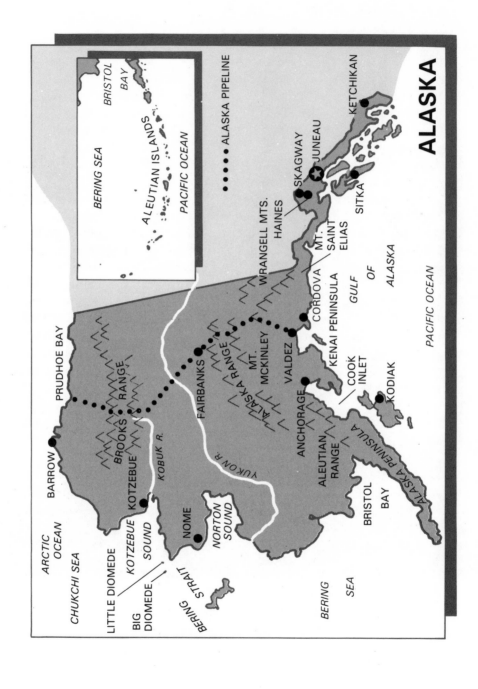

and the men had to spend the winter on an uninhabited island. Half of the crew died during their stay. Vitus Bering died December 8 on the island that is now called Bering Island.

The survivors built a boat from the wreckage of the *St. Peter* and arrived home in the summer of 1742. To stay alive during the winter, the men had eaten the meat of sea otters and covered themselves with the skins. When they brought these back to Russia, the government sent ships to the newfound land for more pelts to sell and trade to other countries.

Some sailors drowned in storms and others were killed by harpoons from Aleut hunters. But by 1745, about 400 Russians had settled on Attu Island at the western end of the Aleutian Islands, and to do this, they had killed many Aleuts. Attu's harbor is called Massacre Bay to commemorate their deaths.

The Russians kept moving east and, by the mid 1760s, they reached the eastern end of the Aleutians. The Aleuts fought them but the Russians were too strong and also had guns. After the Natives sank four boats, the Russians killed 3,000 Aleuts. When one Russian wanted to know how many men could be killed by a single musket, he bound twelve Aleuts in a line and fired. The pellet stopped in the body of the ninth.

The killings might have gone on until all the Aleuts had died. But the Russians needed them to teach them hunting, so they could dominate the fur trade to China. Eventually, the Aleuts and these early Russians learned to depend on each other for survival and the killing stopped. Together, they lived in underground shelters, wore simple fur clothes, and sometimes suffered from lack of food. Forty years after the first Russians reached the Aleutians, the Russians and the Aleuts were still living this way.

RUSSIAN EXPANSION

In 1784, Grigori Ivanovich Shelekhov established a permanent colony at Three Saints Bay, near the present town of Kodiak, and made friends with the Natives. In 1790, he hired Alexander Baranov to manage his fur company.

Baranov started a shipbuilding business and used several of the ships the company built to sail from Kodiak to the mainland of Alaska to begin a new colony. He traded beads, brass, and bottles for land from the Tlingits and built Fort St. Michael in 1799. These Indians were descendants of the people who ambushed Alexei Chirikov's landing parties.

Baranov and his men lived in peace with the Natives. But after he left Fort St. Michael to return to Kodiak, the Tlingits attacked the fort. Armed with guns they had received by trading with English and American sailors, the Indians burned the village and killed most of the colonists. Those who escaped were rescued by American and British ships and brought to Kodiak.

It was 1804 before Baranov could set out to avenge the massacre. By then all Russian activities in Alaska were under the Russian-American Company and Baranov had been made governor of Alaska. When he reached his former colony, a Russian fighting ship was waiting to help him. Day after day, the ship emptied its guns on the village. Tired of waiting aboard ship, Baranov took his Aleuts to fight ashore. He was wounded and his life was saved only because the ship's guns finally drove away the Tlingits.

Baranov built a fort a mile west of the old one and named it New Archangel. This area is now known as Sitka. In 1806, Baranov moved the Russian-American Company from Kodiak to Sitka, which became an important trade center for ships from other countries. Baranov retired in 1818, and thirteen Russian governors followed him in Sitka.

During that time, the Russians continued to explore and develop Alaska. They charted the mouth of the Yukon River, they mined gold and coal on the Kenai Peninsula, and they found oil seeps in Cook Inlet. They also continued to kill fur seals for their pelts until the animal was close to extinction. When conservation measures were established, the Russian-American Company lost so much

Sitka, in 1805, an important trading town and the capital of Russian Alaska

money the government decided to support the company no longer. The government also decided to rid itself of Alaska.

The United States showed interest in the land, and Baron Edouard de Stoeckl was authorized to sell it for $5 million. The American Civil War interrupted talks of the sale, and it was 1866 before de Stoeckl could negotiate seriously with William H. Seward, President Andrew Johnson's secretary of state.

For years, Seward had wanted Alaska and was determined to present an Alaskan deal to Congress before it adjourned at the end of March 1867. On March 14, he offered de Stoeckl $5 million for the property. Then, without waiting for an answer from de Stoeckl, who would certainly have accepted the offer, Seward upped his bid to $5.5 million.

When de Stoeckl saw how much Seward wanted Alaska, he contacted Russia and said he would try to get $6 million. The negotiations and Seward's hurry-up attitude continued until he paid $7.2 million for land he could have bought for $5 million.

The transfer ceremony was held in Sitka on October 18, 1867. The Russian troops marched to the flagpole that flew the Russian flag. Then 200 United States Army men marched to the area. The Russian flag was lowered and the American flag, with thirty-seven stars, was raised. The Russians had established schools, churches, and hospitals and left names and traditions that exist today. They had lived in Alaska for 126 years and, in 1993, Alaska will have belonged to the United States for as long as it had belonged to Russia.

SEWARD'S FOLLY
MAKES GOOD

The Congress in Washington paid little attention to what they called Walrussia, Icebergia, Polaris, Seward's Icebox, and Seward's Folly. To officials in the nation's capital, Alaska seemed primitive, cold, and far away. By 1877, the U.S. Army had gone and the only government officials in Alaska were a customs collector and several postmasters and treasury agents.

GOLD

While Congress generally ignored Alaska, those in search of gold headed for the new frontier. They believed the gold they had found in California washed down in streams that began in the North. In 1880, Joseph Juneau and Richard Harris made a big strike and staked a claim beside the Gastineau Channel. Within days, gold-seekers poured into the area that is now Juneau, the capital of Alaska.

The next big find was in the Canadian Yukon. In August 1896, George Washington Carmack stopped for a drink of water from Bonanza Creek, a tributary of the Klondike River, and saw a gold nugget in the gravel. Those who had been working small claims in Alaska staked Bonanza Creek from end to end. These first comers scooped up most of the fortunes.

There were several popular overland routes to the gold in the Yukon. One, from Skagway, was over the Coast Mountains through White Pass and then down to Lake Bennett. The summit at White Pass was 2,900 feet (900 m). The trip was 40 miles (64 km). Another route was over the Chilkoot Trail from Dyea, an Indian village and trading route, which also led to Lake Bennett. The summit of the Chilkoot Trail was 3,700 feet (1,100 m), but Dyea was only 21 miles (34 km) from the gold discovery. Most of the stampeders chose the shorter route.

They chopped steps into the snow and walked or crawled up on their knees. The climb would not have seemed foolish if they had done it once or twice. But the Canadian government required that each stampeder have a year's supply of food, clothing, and equipment before crossing into Canada. The prospectors carried these on their backs, and many made thirty round-trips before they were allowed to camp beside Lake Bennett to wait for the ice to melt.

Prospectors passed their time making boats from trees. When the ice broke on May 29, 1898, more than 7,000 boats charged down the river to Dawson in Canada. Only a few people struck it rich. By the end of summer, many stampeders were forced to earn a living doing odd jobs or working as laborers on other people's claims. Many headed home, broke.

Dawson was still prospering in 1899 when word came about a gold strike in Nome. By July, 8,000 stampeders jammed onto steamers for the 1,700-mile (2,700-km) journey to Nome. One man spent eight days teaching himself to ride a bike on ice and then rode the bike on river ice and ice-covered ground to Nome, a distance of

A gold miner stands by a sluice box, which drains off the water from the gravel and the gold.

about 1,400 miles (2,200 km). The day he left Dawson the temperature was −20° F (−29° C). On the second day, the temperature dropped to −48° F (−44° C). The tires froze and so did the oil in the bearings. While he waited for the tires and the oil to thaw, a man on ice skates passed him. If the fever struck, people used whatever they could to get to the gold.

When stampeders reached Nome, they found Jafet Lindeberg, Eric Lindblom, and John Brynteson. They had staked a claim in Anvil Creek while most prospectors were still in the Yukon. The three men became millionaires. Hoping to do the same, miners set up tents on a 43-mile (68-km) stretch of shore along the Bering Sea. In 1900 Nome was considered the largest city in Alaska. By 1906 the easy gold had been scooped up and stampeders had moved on.

TERRITORY TO STATEHOOD

Gold brought attention to the District of Alaska. In 1906 it was given a nonvoting delegate to Washington. The Alaskans wanted more. In 1912, a bill written by Judge James Wickersham passed through Congress, and Alaska became a territory. Alaska still wanted more. Their fight for statehood began in 1916, but their requests never made it through the legislative process. It was 1940 before the U.S. government paid serious attention to its territory. That year, the Defense Department began building military bases in Alaska.

On February 11, 1942, two months after World War II started, President Franklin D. Roosevelt authorized the building of a road through Canada into Alaska to provide an overland military supply route to those bases. Construction crews started in March 1942. They worked south from Delta Junction in Alaska, north and south from Whitehorse, and north from Dawson Creek, Canada. The 1,422 miles (2,275 km) of road were completed eight months later, when crews met at Kluane Lake in Yukon Territory, Canada. It was an extraordinary achievement over mountains, rivers, and frozen ground.

In June 1942, while the road was still under construction, the Japanese bombed Dutch Harbor and occupied Attu and Kiska Islands in the Aleutians. It was spring 1943 before American troops retook the islands. The battle raged for eighteen days. On May 29, Japanese charged into the American lines in a final attack. It failed, and the next day the Japanese government announced the fall of Attu.

They had lost 2,350 men and 29 were taken prisoner. The battle had been costly for the United States as well. More than 500 Americans were killed and close to 1,000 were wounded. On August 15, United States troops landed on Kiska, but by then the Japanese soldiers had left the island.

After the war, military people stayed on in Alaska and the population grew. But it grew so slowly that one of the arguments against statehood was the small number of people in the territory. Other arguments were its distance from the other states and the lack of a sound economic base. But when Atlantic Richfield found oil in 1957 at Swanson River on the Kenai Peninsula, Congress listened to arguments for statehood with new interest.

On June 30, 1958, the Senate voted 64–20 to make Alaska a state. As word spread through Alaska, stores closed, bonfires blazed, and church bells rang. In Fairbanks, residents tried to dye the Chena River gold. The water turned green, but nobody seemed to mind. In November, Alaskan voters approved the bill. On January 3, 1959, President Dwight D. Eisenhower signed the papers that proclaimed Alaska a state. The 49-star flag became official on July 4th of that year.

OIL

The first major issue Alaska had to face after becoming a state was the discovery of large oil deposits.

Oil exploration actually began in 1898 at Cook Inlet. In 1902, a significant discovery was made near Cordova. In 1923, President

Warren G. Harding signed an order creating Naval Petroleum Preserve Number 4, a 23-million-acre (9.7-million-hectare) area of Alaska's North Slope. It was not until 1944, when oil shortages during World War II threatened the defense of the United States that drilling at NPR-4 began. Nine oil and gas fields were discovered but there were no significant oil finds. Active exploration was suspended in 1953.

After the North Slope land was transferred from the Department of the Navy to the Department of the Interior, private companies were allowed to bid for the right to drill on the North Slope. In 1968, Atlantic Richfield discovered oil at Prudhoe Bay and brought Alaska to the attention of the world.

In 1970, Alaskan Natives and environmentalists halted development of a pipeline to move the oil by filing lawsuits in the name of the Natives. They claimed the pipeline would destroy the land they and their ancestors had occupied for hundreds of years and, therefore, was rightfully theirs. To avoid long court battles that would have delayed the pipeline, the Alaska Native Claims Settlement Act, which gave Natives 44 million acres (17 million hectares) of land, was signed in 1971.

With the Natives and environmentalists still insisting that the land be protected, more studies were made to learn how oil drilling and spills would affect wildlife. The oil companies also had to overcome the problems of the pipeline route. It would have to cross the Alaska Range and the Chugach Mountains in the south and the Brooks Range in the north before it reached the port of Valdez.

After the Supreme Court refused the appeal by the Natives and environmentalists, Congress passed legislation authorizing construction of the pipeline. President Richard M. Nixon signed an executive order on November 16, 1973 and the building of a road to the North Slope began on April 29, 1974. The first oil left Prudhoe Bay June 20, 1977 and reached Valdez on July 28 at 11:02 P.M. It took 38 days, 12 hours, and 54 minutes.

Alaska pipeline construction overlooking Brooks Mountain Range, about 175 miles (282 km) south of Prudhoe Bay

When the Prudhoe Bay oil field was discovered, it represented one-quarter of the known petroleum reserves in the United States. It produces an average of 1,500,000 barrels of oil a day. The pipeline is 800 miles (1,280 km) long and affects hundreds of river and stream crossings. Almost half of the pipe is buried in areas that have stable soil and rock.

Just over 400 miles (640 km) of pipe are above ground. These sections are laid in a flexible, zigzag pattern and are held by 78,000 supports. The pipes are insulated to keep them from melting the frozen ground and are coated to prevent corrosion. There are hundreds of animal crossings to allow for the annual caribou and moose migrations across Alaska. After the oil reaches Valdez, it is put in storage tanks until it can be loaded on tankers. Some of these boats are longer than three football fields.

Production at Prudhoe Bay is expected to peak during the 1990s and decline after that. In their search, the oil companies continue to drill. They have paid millions of dollars for the right to look for oil and gas in Norton Sound, south of Nome. In 1985 the U.S. secretary of the interior announced that 5.6 million acres (2.1 million hectares) in Bristol Bay would be offered at a lease sale on January 15, 1986. The bay holds the nation's largest salmon and herring fisheries and is the home or migration corridor for more than a million marine mammals, including whales, seals, sea otters, and walruses.

Although the sale was held, litigation was filed on behalf of the state of Alaska, Native organizations, environmental organizations, and fishing organizations. The bids for the land were not opened nor were leases issued. The case has been in court since then. An injunction to stop the sale was upheld, and the issue continues to be debated. Alaska's economy and environment could be damaged as a result of the sale of such large areas to oil companies. But it seems likely that as long as the world uses oil and gas, oil companies will continue their search for oil in Alaska.

CARVING THE PAST
FOR THE FUTURE

When Vitus Bering discovered Alaska in 1741, the Indians, Aleuts, and Eskimos lived within definite areas. There was little mixing of ethnic groups, largely because they spoke different languages.

The Tlingit, the Haida, and the Tsimshian Indians settled in Southeast Alaska. The Athapascan Indians settled in the Alaskan Interior. The Eskimos settled in the northern and western regions. The Aleuts, who are a distant branch of the Eskimos, settled on the Alaska Peninsula, the southwestern coast, and the Aleutian Islands.

The Indians in Southeast Alaska had abundant food. Salmon, deer, bear, and berries permitted easy existence. Because they did not have to follow the wildlife, these Indians lived in villages.

The Athapascan Indians had no permanent homes. They followed migrating moose and caribou and took advantage of the seasonal movement of fish and birds. These provided most of their food, clothing, and shelter. Surplus meat was stored for future use. When game was scarce and the stored food was used up, the Athapascans faced long periods of famine. Sometimes when this happened, the people who were too old or too weak to keep up with the search for food were left to die.

The Alaskan Athapascan Indians are the Northern Athapascans. The Southern Athapascans are the Navajos. Apaches and Hupai are closely related to the Northern Athapascans, primarily through language.

Early Eskimos lived in permanent villages on treeless volcanic rock or tundra. They would scarcely have survived in this environment if they had not been skillful in sea and ice hunting. With only a harpoon in a boat made of driftwood and animal skins, they could capture seals, walruses, and sixty-ton whales. Nothing was wasted. The flesh, blubber, hides, sinews, bones, and teeth of these creatures were used for food, shelter, boats, sleds, clothes, and tools.

The Eskimos lived in skin tents in summer and in partially underground sod and skin houses, supported by driftwood and whalebone, in winter. These dwellings and the smokeless seal-oil lamps that heated them were so expertly made that the temperature inside was comfortable even in the coldest weather.

The Aleuts lived on the chain of islands that stretch westward from the Alaska Peninsula. The original Aleutian houses were communal buildings. Sometimes as many as 150 people lived in one house. Each family had its separate living area partitioned by stakes and grass mats. There were no fireplaces. Heat and light were provided by oil burning lamps.

Thousands of Aleuts were killed by the Russians in the 1700s. But eventually the Aleuts and Russians learned to live together in peace. Because of this commingling, there are few full-blood Aleuts.

For centuries, Natives experienced subsistence living. To qualify for this lifestyle now, Natives must live in rural areas and have a history of living off Alaska's renewable resources. Under subsistence, Natives are allowed to hunt and fish in national parks and animal refuges. But to keep this privilege they must use all parts of the wildlife and fish for food, shelter, fuel, clothing, tools, and transportation. They can also use the non-edible parts to make baskets, carvings, and jewelry to sell as souvenirs. However, the food cannot be sold. It can only be eaten or bartered for personal or family consumption.

All Indians, Eskimos, and Aleuts were made citizens of the United States by the Citizenship Act of June 2, 1924. They asked for medical care, education, and compensation for land they claimed was theirs. But they received little attention from the federal gov-

Above: *an Eskimo dance performed on Nome Beach, 1905*
Left: *a Native boy holds a harpoon twice his height.*

ernment until 1971, when the Alaska Native Claims Settlement Act was signed. This returned to 85,000 Natives 44,000,000 acres (109,000,000 hectares) of land and gave them $962.5 million in compensation for the loss of the lands their ancestors had occupied.

By July 1972, some United States citizens who had at least one-quarter Alaska Native ancestry became shareholders in Native corporations set up to invest the money and help shareholders select land. The money was used for hospitals and public health services and to bring telephone and television facilities to villages and to improve living conditions. Some corporations have made millions of dollars, but some, because of bad investments, are nearly bankrupt.

Adjusting to change has not always been successful. Pressures from traditions and the wish to step into the modern world have been difficult for many Natives. In their search for a place to belong, some have turned to alcohol and drugs and, sometimes, suicide. But others have made the transition successfully. In a state in which jobs are hard to find, Natives work as airplane pilots, mechanics, carpenters, teachers, office workers, senators, and state represen-tatives.

TOTEM POLES

Tradition says the Haida Indians started the art of carving totem poles and that they were the best carvers. The Tlingit Indians were also excellent. But the Haidas were so skillful that the Tlingits some-times hired them to do special poles.

Totems have no religious significance and are not pagan gods or demons. They are story poles that give the history of a particular people. Cedar trees were usually used for totems which were painted with pigments made from soil, berry juice, and spruce sap. Figures were carved with stone, bone, and shell until the Indians acquired steel tools through fur trade with sailors.

Totem poles were made to honor a chief or other outstanding person, to show wealth and power, or to pass on legends.

A totem pole at Sitka
National Historical Park

The Heraldic Pole showed the social standing of the chief or the head of the house and had the family crest carved on the pole. It was attached to the front of the building and usually had an egg-shaped entrance large enough for people to enter.

The Memorial Pole was put up in honor of a deceased chief. The person selected to succeed the dead chief could not assume the wealth, responsibility, and power of his new position until he had erected a pole.

The Ridicule, or Shame, Pole was erected by a chief to discredit a person who broke his word or who behaved in a dishonorable way.

The Potlatch Pole was the largest kind of pole. It was put up during ritualistic or festive observances. Chiefs who wanted to show off their wealth put up poles with many figures and elaborate paintings.

The carving of poles took years and the teamwork of hundreds of people. When they finished, the owner of the pole gave a potlatch. During the celebration, he told the story shown in the carvings while costumed actors dramatized, danced, and sang parts of the story. A potlatch lasted a few days or several weeks and the owner of the pole gave gifts to guests. In return, they helped raise the pole.

After poles were erected, they were seldom repaired. They were left to stand as long as nature would permit, usually about fifty years.

The most extensive collections of totems are at Sitka National Historical Park and at Ketchikan in Totem Bight Park, where there is a replica of a pole to honor Abraham Lincoln. A Tlingit chief who admired the president for freeing the slaves hired a carver to design the memorial pole.

On the totem, the president is wearing his tall hat and his frock coat but his legs are missing. The carver used a picture of Abraham Lincoln to do the totem. The picture had been cut off at the knees and the carver stopped there. The rest of the pole has the usual carvings of animals, including the Raven crest at the base. Because of this crest, the pole is also called the Proud Raven Pole. The original Lincoln carving is preserved at the State Museum in Juneau.

WATER HIGHWAYS
AND MOUNTAINS

The Coast Mountains between Alaska and Canada form a natural barrier that makes road construction to Southeast Alaska difficult. Skagway and Haines are the only cities in this area that have roads leading to other cities. The rest of the communities can be reached only by small planes or ferries. Ferries are the buses, vans, and trains of Southeast Alaska. They carry passengers, personal belongings, cars, and trucks.

Because the region is protected from northerly winds by mountains and warmed by the current from the Pacific Ocean, it has the warmest temperatures in Alaska. It also has the most rain.

Almost all of Southeast Alaska is in the Tongass National Forest and is protected by state and federal agencies. Important cities in this region are Juneau, Sitka, and Skagway.

JUNEAU

More than a hundred years ago, two prospectors named Joseph Juneau and Richard Harris found gold nuggets the size of peas near the Gastineau Channel and staked claims. Harris named the town Harrisburg in his honor. But in 1881, prospectors became angry with Harris for staking multiple claims and renamed it Juneau.

In 1912, the district of Alaska became a territory and the government offices were moved from Sitka to Juneau. After Alaska became a state, many people wanted to move the capital to Willow or to Anchorage. However, Alaskans voted against spending the millions of dollars it would cost to build a new capital. With the news that the government offices would stay in Juneau, houses, businesses, and shops sprouted along the hills and twisting narrow streets.

The population of Juneau is 20,000 and it is still growing. This has created suburbs and more miles of roads, but they all end in a loop. There is no road that leads out of the capital of the largest state in the United States.

SITKA

Sitka was the capital of Russian Alaska. Its influence shows in the new St. Michael's Russian Orthodox Cathedral. The original church, built in the mid-1800s, was destroyed by fire in 1966. Almost all the sacred images and paintings that had been brought from Russia were saved. They are now in the new cathedral built in 1976.

Beyond the church is Castle Hill. A Tlingit village stood on top of this hill until Russians destroyed the Indian houses and built a home for Alexander Baranov. The residence was so large that it became known as Baranov's Castle and the hilltop as Castle Hill.

There, on October 18, 1867, Russians and Americans transferred the ownership of Alaska. While cannons boomed, the Russian flag was lowered and the American flag was raised. Several cannons still stand on Castle Hill, but Baranov's Castle is no longer there. It was destroyed by fire in 1894.

Most of Sitka is under the protection of the Sitka National Historical Park.

SKAGWAY

William Moore was the first white man to settle in Skagway. He staked a mining claim in October 1887 and then built a cabin and a wharf and called the area Mooresville.

The Alaska State Capitol building in Juneau

The gold discovery in the Yukon brought prospectors and trouble. The miners ignored Moore's claim, and a group of surveyors laid out the town they initially called Skaguay. Moore went to court and eventually received money for the property he had lost.

In 1898, Michael J. Heney began building the White Pass and Yukon Route Railroad to take prospectors to the gold in Canada. By the time the 110-mile (176-km) railroad was finished in 1900, thousands of miners had moved north to stake claims in Nome. The number of Skagway residents fell from 10,000 to hundreds. But the railroad kept the community going by transporting food and supplies from Skagway to Canada.

Tourists now keep the town alive. The highway that opened in 1978, the ferries that started operating in 1963, and tour boats that land at William Moore's wharf bring thousands of people during the summer months. Seven blocks in the center of the town are part of the Klondike Gold Rush National Historical Park. The area has been restored to the way it looked when the town was known as Skaguay.

SOUTHCENTRAL
AND INTERIOR

The southcentral and interior regions have many communities of fewer than a hundred people. Anchorage and Fairbanks, the most populated cities in the state, are here. Major highways run between Anchorage and Fairbanks, and the Alaska Railroad connects the two cities. This makes them important to the private businesses that have helped the cities look and function like cities in the rest of the United States.

These areas have forests, valleys, and farmlands. The Matanuska Valley has the most farms. The growing season averages only 110 days, but during those days there are up to 19 hours of sunlight. Dairy farming is the dominant income source. Farmers also grow vegetables, fruits, and grains to feed livestock. The vegetables and fruits are generally average. But some farmers compete to grow record-sized crops. Cabbages grown in Matanuska Valley have weighed over 70 pounds (31 kg) and strawberries are sometimes as big as a child's fist.

Many people in the Valley are descendants of farmers who came to the area in 1935 when the federal government relocated 204 families after drought struck their farms during the Depression.

ANCHORAGE

Anchorage was founded in 1914, when it was chosen as the midpoint construction headquarters for the Alaska Railroad. A tent city

—35

sprang up along Ship Creek, now the center of the city, and settlers built homes and businesses. By 1915, the area was known as Anchorage. The city had fewer than 8,000 residents at the beginning of World War II. But military bases brought in thousands of people, and by 1950 there were more than 40,000 living in Anchorage and its suburbs.

FAIRBANKS

Fairbanks started in 1901 when E. T. Barnette set up a trading post along the banks of the Chena River, which flows through present-day Fairbanks. The following year, Felix Pedro, an Italian prospector, found gold in the nearby hills. This discovery started a stampede of miners and Fairbanks was incorporated as a city in 1903. It was named for Senator Charles Fairbanks of Indiana, who later became vice president under Theodore Roosevelt.

When the gold ran out, so many people left that the town almost disappeared. But the building of the Alaska Railroad and military bases turned Fairbanks into one of the most important cities in the state. The University of Alaska at Fairbanks is the northernmost university in North America. It has an agricultural experiment station and a geophysical institute and conducts programs on Alaskan Native languages, among other topics.

Fairbanks holds the annual World Eskimo-Indian Olympics. Athletes come from all over Alaska to test their strength and endurance. The sports include the greased-pole walk, the four-man carry, and the knuckle hop. During the greased-pole walk, contestants try to walk down a 6-inch (15-cm) diameter log smeared with grease. The four-man carry is a Native-style weight-lifting contest. Four men weighing a total of 600 pounds (272 kg) cling to the front, back, and sides of a contestant. During the knuckle hop athletes move forward by hopping on their curled fists. The knuckle hop is so grueling that it is the last event of the games.

Some Natives who come to take part or watch the Olympics perform their dances at Alaskaland, a frontier-style theme park. It

An aerial view of Anchorage

has a gold-rush town, a mining valley, a native village, and a stern-wheeler which used to run on Alaska's inland waters. The 40-acre (16-hectare) park was built in 1967 to celebrate the centennial of Alaska's purchase from Russia.

VALDEZ

Old Valdez was a small gold-rush harbor where miners could rest and buy supplies before they headed north to the gold fields. The city has an ice-free port and entry by highway to the interior. Although the road is now paved, it started as a pack trail for the miners and then became a wagon road for supplies. During World War II it was connected to the Alaska Highway.

In 1964, much of the community was washed away by a seismic tidal wave created by an earthquake that struck the southern region of Alaska. Residents wanted to rebuild on the same land but geologists told them the sandy soil was not safe. The residents moved the buildings that had survived the earthquake to more stable ground 4 miles (6.4 km) west and started building their city.

New Valdez was a small town of low ranch-style buildings until it was chosen as the southern end of the trans-Alaska pipeline. In the mid-1970s thousands of workers and their families arrived in Valdez. There were not enough houses for them, and people camped in tents throughout the city and its outskirts. Schools were crowded and prices soared at the town's two grocery stores. But salaries were high and people kept coming.

NORTHERN, WESTERN,
AND SOUTHWESTERN

No place on earth has harsher weather than the areas that border the Arctic Ocean and the Bering Sea. Winds from Siberia blow snow that often becomes miniature icicles before it reaches Alaska. For more than two months a year, the sun does not rise above the horizon and the Arctic is in darkness. The snow and ice that cover the ground eight months a year and the cloud-wrapped sky create feelings of isolation in a world of monotony. Except for a few stands of trees in river gravel, the area is treeless.

In the southwestern region, the Aleutian Islands also have few trees. Winds blow almost continuously through this area. Shemya, on the western end of the Islands, has experienced winds estimated at 140 miles (224 km) per hour. The weather bureau says "estimated" because the wind recorder pen used was able to record statistics only up to 128 miles (204 km) per hour.

Frequent rainstorms and fogs hide the sun for much of the year. These conditions are the result of the clash of air over the Pacific Ocean warmed by the Japanese current and the frigid Bering Sea. The combination of warm and cold creates storms that affect the weather in most of the North American continent.

The United States owns Little Diomede in the Bering Sea. The island is 2.4 miles (3.84 km) from Big Diomede, which is owned by the Soviet Union. People on Little Diomede and Big Diomede used to visit each other. But during the 1950s the Soviet Union cleared its island of civilians and now uses it to watch the coast of Alaska. Little Diomede is the closest United States land to Soviet Union land.

BARROW

Barrow was sighted in 1826 by an English explorer who named it for a secretary of the British admiralty. With about 2,000 residents, it is the largest Eskimo village in the world.

Barrow was a quiet community until oil was discovered at Prudhoe Bay 200 miles (320 km) east. Within months the area was filled with workers whose job it was to get oil out of the ground and find ways to ship it to markets. These people were quickly followed by natural scientists whose jobs were to study how oil drilling and oil spills would affect wildlife.

The oil companies hired workers from all over the world, including teams of Natives from Barrow. They flew them to Prudhoe Bay for two weeks of work, then flew them back to Barrow and picked up new crews. The workers then had two weeks off to hunt and fish for their families.

Barrow became a boom town, as the gold strike cities had been years earlier. But instead of putting up tents and shacks, the oil companies put up houses, office buildings, and stores. When the oil began to flow in 1977, the number of workers dwindled, but they left a modern community.

There are televisions, telephones, and homes heated with natural gas, and there is the northernmost supermarket in the United States. There is also the largest school district in the country. The $62.5-million public school in Barrow services the North Slope Borough, which has eleven villages and is the size of California. The school, built with money from the Prudhoe Bay oil, opened in 1983, the same year the state government collected $140 million in taxes from the oil fields.

Despite these changes, many villagers continue to hunt and fish for their food. Some do it because transportation costs make food expensive. Others do it because it is a tradition handed down through thousands of years.

KOTZEBUE

Kotzebue is near the land bridge that once joined Asia and North America and dates back 6,000 years. It is named for Otto von Kotzebue, a Russian navigator who spotted the area in the early 1800s.

The largest building in the community is the Museum of the Arctic. It has Eskimo artifacts, handicrafts, and a life-size diorama of Arctic wildlife. In addition to the culture display, hosts also give dance programs. The drums used to accompany the dancers are made of walrus stomach stretched tight and attached to a driftwood rim. After the dances, hosts demonstrate the blanket toss.

The "blanket" is a walrus or caribou hide with rope handles held by an even number of people. By pulling together, they can rocket the blanket rider as high as 20 feet (6 m). Now it is done in fun. But years ago, the blanket toss, which works like a trampoline, was used by Eskimo hunters to search for food. The person who was tossed was the "spotter" and it was his job to spot animals and give hunters directions.

Kotzebue's Main Street hugs the beach of Kotzebue Sound. During the brief summer, the sound is filled with boats and fish nets. Seal, walrus, and whale meat hang on racks to dry. During the 24 hours of summer daylight everyone works to gather and prepare food for the winter.

When the weather turns cold, workers move from outside work to inside work such as carving ivory from walrus tusks or weaving baskets with baleen from whales. These handicrafts are sold at shops or in the Museum of the Arctic. Workers also process jade brought from the slopes of Jade Mountain near the Kobuk River.

In the factory, a cavernlike room without windows, workers cut and polish jade, which will eventually be used for rings, necklaces, tabletops, and souvenirs.

There is one full-grown tree in Kotzebue. A hand-scrawled sign with the words "Kotzebue National Forest" stands in front of an evergreen which had been flown in by military personnel stationed at a now closed base. They planted the tree, nourished it, and coaxed it to grow in the tundra, where trees are only inches high at maturity. This is a local joke and is typical of the several communities where trees are unusual.

NOME

As does Barrow and Kotzebue, Nome has a large Eskimo population. Until 1960, most of the Natives lived on King Island, where they had lived for centuries. Although the Eskimos used to come to Nome in the summer to fish and pick berries, they always returned to King Island. However, when the Bureau of Indian Affairs condemned their school building in 1959, the villagers moved to the Nome area permanently. Many still go to King Island to hunt and visit their houses, which still cling to the cliffs.

During World War II, the federal government built an air base in Nome. The base was the last stop for planes the United States supplied to the Soviet Union to help them fight the Germans during World War II. That base forms part of today's airport.

A yearly highlight is the Iditarod Trail Sled Dog Race. The race begins in Anchorage and ends in the middle of Front Street, Nome's main street. In 1985, Libby Riddles became the first woman to win the race, which is officially described as 1,049 miles (1,700 km) long but is closer to 1,200 miles (1,900 km). Susan Butcher won the race in 1986. She broke the record of 12 days, 8 hours, 45 minutes, and 2 seconds established in 1981 by Rick Swenson. Butcher's official time was 11 days, 15 hours, 6 minutes. And in 1987, she broke her own record. She covered the distance in 11

Visitors to wintertime Alaska enjoy a dogsled ride.

days, 2 hours, 5 minutes, and 13 seconds, approximately 13 hours faster than in 1986.

The race follows part of the old dog-team mail route. It crosses two mountain ranges, follows part of the Yukon River, runs through several villages, and crosses the ice on Norton Sound before reaching Nome. During the old-time mail runs, carriers slept in roadhouses or in homes of friends along the way—or even slept with their dogs. There are no home stops during the race. Racers depend entirely on their dogs for companionship and warmth. Mail is delivered by plane now. But the mail route received world attention in 1925 when sled dog drivers brought diphtheria serum a distance of 658 miles (1,053 km) by dog trail. The medicine ended the epidemic that had threatened the city's population.

KODIAK

The city of Kodiak was established by the Russians, and Alexander Baranov used it as his headquarters until he moved to Sitka. The building in which he stored furs to sell or trade is now a museum.

Kodiak boomed during World War II, when 25,000 American troops lived at Fort Abercrombie, 8 miles (12.8 km) away. After the war, much of the military left and Kodiak became a quiet fishing community. The downtown district was destroyed by seismic waves that hit the island of Kodiak after the 1964 Alaskan earthquake. The area was rebuilt and the waterfront is now lined with businesses that serve mostly boaters and fishermen.

Z

PARKLANDS
AND
WILDLIFE REFUGES

On December 2, 1980, President Jimmy Carter signed the Alaska National Interest Lands Conservation Act (ANILCA). This gave Alaska nearly 103 million acres (41 million hectares) of national parks, wildlife refuges, wilderness areas, and rivers. If all this were put together, it would fill the state of California.

The following are some of the parks and wildlife refuges that preserve the natural, historical, and cultural features of Alaska.

SOUTHEASTERN

Tongass National Forest, established in 1907, is the largest national forest in the United States. The park covers almost all of Southeast Alaska and has more than 16 million acres (6.4 million hectares) of mountains, fjords, and glaciers. Included in Tongass National Forest are Admiralty Island National Monument, 15 miles (24 km) west of Juneau, and Misty Fjords National Monument, adjacent to the Canadian border.

Glacier Bay National Park was a 100-mile (160-km) long, 20-mile (32-km) wide ice block that was 4,000-feet (1,222 m) deep around 200 years ago. Then more rain fell than snow and the ice began to melt, forming fjords and the 60-mile (96-km) long Glacier Bay. The Bay has experienced at least four major glacier advances and four major retreats. Because of this frequent movement, scientists use the area as an outdoor laboratory for glacial research.

Klondike Gold Rush National Historical Park includes most of the buildings in Skagway, the ghost town of Dyea, the Chilkoot Trail, and White Pass. These areas all commemorate the gold rush of 1898.

Sitka National Historical Park is a forest sanctuary for native plants. Its cultural center holds classes on Tlingit history and handiwork. The park contains a historic Indian fish camp and Alexander Baranov's settlement. It also preserves the site of the 1804 battle that marked the last major resistance of the Tlingit Indians to Russian colonization.

SOUTHCENTRAL AND INTERIOR

Denali National Park and Preserve is 237 miles (380 km) north of Anchorage and 121 miles (194 km) south of Fairbanks. It was called Mount McKinley National Park until the name was changed to Denali in 1980. Denali is the Athapascan Indian word that means Great One. The "great one" is Mount McKinley, which is the highest peak in North America. The park is about the size of the state of Massachusetts.

Yukon Flats Refuge Wildlife Preserve is the most northerly point of the Yukon River. Here, the river breaks away from canyons and spreads out 200 miles (320 km). In the spring, millions of migrating birds from four continents come to the flats.

Yukon-Charley Rivers National Preserve contains much of the Yukon River and all of the Charley River. The Yukon is gray with glacial silt, while the smaller Charley is crystal clear. The cliffs and bluffs along the rivers provide nesting habitats for peregrine falcons. Old cabins and relics from the Gold Rush dot the preserve.

NORTHERN, WESTERN, AND SOUTHWESTERN

Kobuk Valley National Park has 25 square miles (40 sq km) of sand dunes that are an exposed portion of a dune field formed by glaciers

Hikers at Denali National Park and Preserve

during the Ice Age. In this desert of the Arctic, summer temperatures reach 90° F (33° C). The Kobuk River channel is one of North America's most important archaeological sites. It contains many layers of artifacts dating back 12,000 years.

The Bering Land Bridge National Preserve is a remnant of the land bridge that connected Asia with North America. More than 100 species of migratory birds can be seen in the preserve along with occasional seals, walruses, and whales.

Alaska Maritime National Wildlife Refuge is made up of more than 2,400 islands, rocks, and reefs on the state's southwestern coast. About 75 percent of Alaska's marine birds use the refuge. Each species has its nesting site, which allows many different kinds of birds to use the small area of land. Thousands of sea lions, seals, walruses, and sea otters also live in the refuge.

WILDLIFE AT
THE TOP OF
THE WORLD

The climate, the ecological conditions, and the short growing season for food make year-round living in Alaska difficult for many animals. The large numbers of animals, fish, and birds that you read or hear about are usually seasonal and are seen mostly during migration, breeding, and spawning.

LAND ANIMALS

The following animals usually migrate within Alaska:

BLACK BEARS—With an average weight of 190 pounds (86 kg), black bears are the smallest of North American bears. Their color varies from jet black to white, but black is the most common color seen in Alaska. They have poor eyesight, but their hearing and sense of smell are well developed. In the spring, when they come out of hibernation, their main food is freshly sprouted green vegetation. In the summer, they eat meat and fish. And in the fall they prefer blueberries and roots before they return to their winter hibernation.

BROWN/GRIZZLY BEARS—Until recently, the brown and grizzly bears were listed as separate species. However, scientists have now classified them as a single species. These bears are found throughout most of Alaska. They eat berries, grass, and roots. They also eat fish and sometimes line streams to fish for salmon with

*In Alaska, where wildlife abounds
in the vast wilderness areas of
the state, it is not unusual to
catch sight of a brown or grizzly
bear resting along the roadside.*

their paws. Males can weigh as much as 1,400 pounds (636 kg) and are the largest carnivorous animals on earth.

POLAR BEARS—Polar and brown bears evolved from a common ancestor and they are still closely related. Their white coat with water-repellent hairs and fur over large areas of their paws make it possible for polar bears to live on ice. Mature males weigh as much as 1,200 pounds (545 kg). They are found on the icy edges of the Arctic Ocean and the Bering Sea. Their main food is the ringed seal.

BISON—The bison in Alaska are descendants of bison brought from Montana in 1928. Full-grown males weigh more than 2,000 pounds (910 kg). Alaska's bison do not stay in herds. They migrate singly or in small groups. They are grazing animals and their diet is made up of grasses. The limit of grass ranges keeps the state's bison population small.

CARIBOU—These animals are large members of the deer family. Males weigh about 400 pounds (182 kg). Caribou travel in herds and, as do most herd animals, they keep moving to find food. This tends to prevent overgrazing which, in turn, preserves food supplies.

MOOSE—The moose is the largest member of the deer family in the world, and the Alaskan moose is the largest of all moose. Male animals weigh as much as 1,500 pounds (680 kg). Moose were an important source of food, clothing, and tools to the Athapascan Indians in central Alaska. They are still used for food by many Natives, and hunters kill more than ten thousand moose each year for meat. Their large number ensures their survival in Alaska.

MUSK OX—Musk oxen have changed little since the Ice Age and are perfectly adapted to live in their Arctic environment. Scientists classify them with sheep and goats. In the 1800s, the original Alaskan musk ox disappeared because of overhunting. In 1930, thirty-four musk oxen were captured in Greenland and brought to Fairbanks. Five years later, the surviving musk oxen and their calves were released on Nunivak Island in the Bering Sea. Since then, musk oxen have been transplanted to limited areas of Alaska.

Some of the small animals in Alaska are the beaver, coyote, fox, lynx, mink, muskrat, marmot, and pika. Fossil remains show that the pika, which weighs only 5 ounces (142 g) as an adult, came to North America over the land bridge 15 million years ago.

SEA MAMMALS

WHALES—Gray whales are the only large whales that can regularly be seen along Alaskan shores. They are found in the North Pacific Ocean and the Arctic Ocean. Some of these migrate between Baja California and the Bering and Chukchi seas—a round-trip of more than 10,000 miles (16,000 km). Other large whales in Alaska are the blue, bowhead, fin, humpback, and killer.

SEALS—The commonest and most widespread seal in the Arctic is the ringed seal. These seals usually live in the northern Bering, Chukchi, and Beaufort seas, but they have been seen as far south as the Aleutian Islands. Other mammals that live in the coastal waters of northern and western Alaska are bearded seals, ribbon seals, spotted seals, sea lions, and sea otters.

WALRUSES—Walruses are the largest pinnipeds in the Arctic. The flesh is used for food, the skin for boat coverings, and the intestines are occasionally used by Eskimos for rain gear and windows. Walruses are found in shallow water near ice or land. Most of them migrate between Bristol Bay on the west coast of Alaska to Point Barrow on the northern coast. Adult males weigh up to 3,000 pounds (1,360 kg).

FISH

Some of the smaller fish in Alaskan waters are the halibut, herring, pike, trout, and salmon. There are five kinds of salmon in Alaska. The king salmon is the state fish and is the most sought-after for food. A female can lay as many as 14,000 eggs at one time. Like other salmon, the king hatches in fresh water, spends part of its life in the ocean, then spawns in fresh water. All king salmon die after spawning. They have a life span of seven years and can weigh as much as 90 pounds (40 kg).

BIRDS

More than 400 species of birds have been spotted in Alaska by bird-watchers. The birds migrate from all parts of the world. The arctic tern travels the farthest. It flies more than 22,000 miles (35,000 km) during its flight from the Antarctic to Alaska and back to the Antarctic.

Because the best way to preserve wildlife species is to protect their habitats, the Alaskan government has made this a top priority. A recent project was the installation of artificial islands in the Copper River Delta.

The environment in this area changed after the 1964 earthquake. Repeated shock waves lifted the delta an average of 6 feet (1.8 m) above pre-quake levels and allowed coyotes, bears, and wolves to reach nesting birds. The artificial islands make this difficult and often impossible. The bird population in the delta, especially the dusky Canada goose and the trumpeter swan, has increased since the project began.

Several years ago, bald eagles were in danger for a different reason. Timber harvesting in the Tongass National Forest threatened their nesting territories. Biologists, foresters, and engineers worked together to save the nesting areas while tree-cutting continued. The project was so successful that there are now enough eagles in Southeast Alaska to allow them to be released in other states.

Some of the other birds in Alaska are the crane, duck, grouse, loon, ptarmigan, and puffin. Puffins have stout bodies, short wings, orange or red webbed feet, and a bright yellow beak with a red tip. Their comical image has been reproduced on clothes, jewelry, mugs, and greeting cards, making them the most popular seabird in Alaska.

TALL MOUNTAINS
AND
SHORT TREES

MOUNTAINS

The three highest mountain peaks in the United States are in Alaska. They are McKinley South Peak, 20,320 feet (6,100 m); McKinley North Peak, 19,470 feet (5,900 m), both in the Alaska Range; and St. Elias, 18,008 feet (5,500 m) on the Alaska-Canada border.

Mount McKinley was named in 1896 for William McKinley, who was elected president of the United States that year. Vitus Bering named St. Elias. It was the first land he saw during his exploration of the Alaskan coast.

The longest mountain ranges in Alaska are the Brooks Range in the north, which separates the arctic region from central Alaska. The Alaska Range is in the south. The southwestern extension of the Alaska Range becomes the Aleutian Range and the Aleutian Islands. Shorter mountain ranges include the Chugach Mountains and the Wrangell Mountains which merge with the St. Elias Mountains.

The position of the Brooks and Alaska ranges causes the extreme high and low temperatures in central Alaska. Also, because the Brooks Range blocks moisture from the Arctic Ocean and the Alaska Range blocks moisture from the Pacific Ocean, central Alaska receives about the same amount of moisture as some U.S. desert areas.

PERMAFROST

Permafrost is a contraction of the words "permanent frost." It is ground that stays frozen for two or more years. In northern Alaska this frozen ground reaches a depth of 2,000 feet (600 m).

Permafrost forms a seal that does not allow water to be absorbed. For much of the year the water that falls in the form of rain and snow is locked in ice. In the summer, a layer of soil thaws and becomes spongy, but the permafrost beneath remains at below-freezing temperatures.

Permafrost covers most of the northern third of the state. Isolated patches also exist over the central area. There is no permafrost in the southeastern or southcentral regions or on the Alaska Peninsula and the Aleutian Islands.

TUNDRA

Tundra comes from the Finnish word for "barren land," and refers to the area north of the timberline. Tundra covers about 30 percent of the land in Alaska. Precipitation in some of these areas is as low as 5 inches (12.7 cm) a year. This is similar to the rainfall in the desert areas of the rest of the states. Yet, because low temperatures and permafrost prevent evaporation and absorption of the moisture, the ground is always damp. The tundra is therefore characterized by bogs and marshes. Vegetation consists of lichen, mosses, and flowering plants. Trees and shrubs also grow in the tundra, but they are only a few inches high at maturity. The dwarfed growth is due to shallow roots that cannot penetrate the permafrost.

GLACIERS

Glaciers form in high mountains when winter snowfall is more than summer melt. The weight of the accumulating snow causes ice crystals to fuse together and form glacial ice. This ice has the ability

to flow. Some glaciers, however, do not move for long periods of time, while others advance and retreat. When the ice builds, the glacier advances and covers the land in its path, destroying vegetation. When the ice melts, the glacier retreats and leaves boulders, gravel, sand, and silt. In time, plants, shrubs, and finally trees grow there and provide shelter and food for wildlife.

The Hubbard Glacier, an 80-mile (128-km) river of ice that begins in Canada and ends at Yukutat Bay in southeast Alaska, has made ten major advances and retreats since the Ice Age ended about 10,000 years ago. These movements did not cause serious problems. However, in 1986, Hubbard advanced so fast and so far that by June, the glacier and its rocky moraine had sealed off Russell Fjord. This changed the saltwater bay into a lake filled by rain and glacial melt. This newly formed body of water was renamed Russell Lake.

The ecological changes threatened fisheries and timber resources and trapped seals and porpoises that had been feeding in the saltwater inlet. This rapid loss of their natural habitat endangered the mammals, and rescuers tried to help them get back into salt water. They did not succeed. However, in September, icebergs began breaking off the glacier and in early October Hubbard's dam broke. The water gushing from Russell Lake released the trapped animals and eased the possible danger to the fisheries and timber.

The 100,000 glaciers in Alaska cover 3 percent of the state. They include the smallest glaciers, which have no names, to the biggest glacier, which is called Malaspina Glacier. Malaspina is about the size of Rhode Island.

A cruise ship off an Alaskan glacier. With all its beautiful scenery, Alaska is a popular choice for travelers.

TREES, PLANTS, AND FLOWERS

Northern and western Alaska, the Alaska Peninsula, and the Aleutian Islands are almost treeless. The southeastern region, however, has dense forests. Some of the species of trees in Alaska are aspen, birch, cedar, cottonwood, hemlock, maple, and spruce.

Wild fruit bushes provide blueberries, cranberries, raspberries, strawberries, and crab apples.

Flowers include the fireweed, forget-me-not, iris, poppy, arctic larkspur, and the tundra rose.

Of the 1,500 plant species that grow in Alaska, lichen is the most important to vegetation and animals. It is the earth's longest living plant and grows on tree bark and rocks. Lichen is among the first growth that appears in the silt left by glaciers. Lichen is also the life food for reindeer and caribou. For nine months of the year, these animals can survive on the frozen lichen if nothing else is available.

10

LIVING IN ALASKA

Just as in most other states, the way people live depends a great deal on whether they live in cities or in small towns or villages. Some services available in urban situations are often not available in rural areas such as the Bush. The Bush is any part of Alaska that has no access road and sometimes has no schools, no television, and no phone. Most areas of Alaska, however, do have television and phone service from the Alaska Communication System.

On October 27, 1982, Alascom launched a satellite from Cape Canaveral, Florida. With this satellite, a telephone call from Alaska often travels 100,000 miles (160,000 km). The signal goes from the ground to the satellite, then down to Anchorage, Fairbanks, or Juneau, back to the satellite, and finally to receiving stations in other states. This service is available to communities that have twenty-five people or more. Satellites also give live or same-day television programs to 90 percent of Alaska's population.

Costs for these services are high. So are prices for food and houses. Shipping and storing of goods double the price of everything from furniture to ice cream cones. Salaries for workers are above-average to help pay the higher expenses, but jobs are hard to find.

INDUSTRIES AND JOBS

City, state, and federal governments employ more people in Alaska than does any industry. This does not include personnel stationed at military bases throughout the state. Despite these government jobs, unemployment is high even for people who have lived in the state for many years.

Three leading industries in Alaska are:

PETROLEUM—The research, exploring, drilling, and refining of oil and natural gas have been responsible for much of the state's income and population growth.

COMMERCIAL FISHING—Commercial fishing is extensive in the Bering Sea, along the Aleutian Islands, and in the Gulf of Alaska. Salmon has been the main product, but shrimp is gaining in importance. The value of the fish caught in and around Alaska is greater than that of fish caught in any other state. The volume is second only to Louisiana. There are few regulations on commercial fishing in Alaska, but there are a number of laws to protect whales. These restrictions, however, allow whaling by Alaskan Indians, Aleuts, and Eskimos under strict subsistence guidelines.

TOURISM—The number of out-of-state visitors has increased for several years. They create summer jobs for many Alaskans and for workers from other states. More than 1,500 businesses make most of their money from sales to tourists.

Other industries are commercial timber and pulp mills, which are located mostly in southeastern Alaska; mining of coal, copper, gold, and platinum; and farming in Delta Junction and in the Matanuska and Tanana valleys. The growth of industries in Alaska is hindered by weather conditions and lack of good transportation.

TRANSPORTATION

For hundreds of years sleds, pulled by dogs, were used to hunt and fish, to haul mail, and to travel short or long distances. The

*Commercial salmon fishing
in southern Alaska*

sleds are still used by some Alaskans in the Bush and by Park Rangers to patrol hard-to-reach areas of parks and preserves. But most people have switched from dogsleds to snowmobiles for short trips and to airplanes for long ones.

There are almost 10,000 registered planes in the state. These private planes are used to take people to work, to school, or to visit friends and relatives. Most of the planes are small and are equipped with wheels, skis, or floats, depending on the weather and the condition of the landing areas. In winter, iced-over streams, lakes, and some rivers become landing strips for planes and highways for trucks that carry supplies to the many areas that have no roads.

The only road that connects Alaska to the lower 48 states is the Alaska Highway. For a short time, this road was called the Alcan Highway and ran 1,422 miles (2,275 km) from Dawson Creek, Canada, to Delta Junction, Alaska, where it hooked onto the Richardson Highway for 98 miles (160 km). The Richardson Highway is 368 miles (600 km), which includes the 98 miles (160 km) it shares with the Alaska Highway, and runs from Fairbanks to Valdez. Only two other highways are more than 300 miles (480 km) long. These are the Glenn Highway and the George Parks Highway.

The Department of Transportation has only 14,000 miles (22,400 km) of highways, which includes the 1,416 miles (2,265 km) of the Marine Highway System. This system, which began in 1963, is not concrete, gravel, or dirt. It is water. A fleet of nine ferries serves

Above: *private planes, like this one, often take the place of cars and buses.* Below: *the Alaska State Troopers, Department of Public Safety, use high powered patrol boats, like* Enforcer, *for police work.*

the southeastern and southwestern regions, which have no conventional roads.

The Alaska Railroad is the northernmost railroad in North America. It has 470 miles (750 km) of track that begins in Seward and ends in Fairbanks. The railroad offers year-round passenger, freight, and vehicle transportation. The train runs daily from the middle of May to the middle of September. In the winter, it runs once a week between Anchorage and Fairbanks.

The railroad offers flag-stop service to people who live in remote areas along the tracks. Because of these unscheduled stops and because freight trains have the right-of-way, passenger trains seldom reach their destination on time.

Alaska has thousands of miles of streams, lakes, and rivers. During the summer, boats are an important means of getting people and supplies to isolated areas that cannot be reached by other means of transportation.

HOUSING

Eskimos in Alaska do not live in igloos. They never did. It was the Canadian Eskimos who used snow and ice to build their houses. However, Alaskans have built emergency snowhouses for survival on long journeys or when hunting parties were caught by storms. Today, some Alaskans live in sod houses. In areas where snow piles up, doors are cut in roofs. But most people live in houses similar to those in other states.

The climate affects how buildings are erected. New structures in the Arctic are perched on metal frames. If buildings were not elevated, the heat from inside would melt the permafrost below and cause the structures to tilt. Older houses which were not built on stilts now have slanted floors and walls and eventually will fall.

Many homes throughout the state are put together by prefabricated parts that are flown in or brought in on barges. Some houses, especially in Bush areas, are made of logs.

In warmer regions, structures are painted bright colors. In colder areas, the wood is treated to keep it from rotting and then often left unpainted. This is especially true in the Arctic, where winds sometimes blow frozen snow that damages paint.

Many homes have food freezers, but some people still preserve food in ice cellars dug in the permafrost. Food is also kept in caches. These are storage cabins on stilts that protect the food from animals.

During the winter, water pipes are often drained to keep them from bursting. In many areas, ice blocks, chopped from frozen lakes, are melted for drinking, cooking, and washing. Homes are heated with natural gas, oil, or wood. To keep heat from escaping, houses are chinked. This is done by creating clouds of steam. The moisture from the steam leaks through cracks in the walls and windows and seals the house for the winter.

SCHOOLS

There are more than 90,000 students in kindergarten through twelfth grade in 550 public schools, 60 private and denominational schools, and 20 Bureau of Indian Affairs day schools. The Bureau of Indian Affairs day schools are in remote villages. Some of these have only one to five graduates a year and may have one teacher for all children from kindergarten to eighth grade.

Until 1976, students who wanted to attend high school had to go outside their village. Now, communities that have one or more people of high school age must offer high school studies. A student named Molly Hootch is responsible for this law. She won a court decree that said she and all other Alaskan children were entitled to continue their education in their villages.

Required courses for graduation are language arts, social studies, math, science, and physical education. In addition, some schools offer traditional Native culture classes that include sewing, cooking, animal trapping, and sled making. They also have alcohol and drug abuse curriculums.

Children from ages seven to sixteen must be enrolled in classes. But they do not have to attend class. They can study at home through the Centralized Correspondence Study Program, which many choose because of extreme weather conditions and lack of roads.

Alaska has two private colleges—Alaska Pacific University and Sheldon Jackson College. There is also a statewide university system. The largest campus is in Fairbanks. There is also an extensive community college system.

WEATHER

Alaska covers so much area that the state has several kinds of weather. The southeast has the mildest and wettest, the interior the dryest and coldest, and the arctic and the Aleutian Islands the foggiest and windiest.

The coldest temperature ever recorded in Alaska was $-80°$ F ($-62°$ C) at Prospect Creek on January 23, 1971. The highest recorded temperature was 100° F (38° C) at Fort Yukon on June 27, 1915. The greatest annual rain and snow fell in 1976 at MacLeod Harbor on Montague Island in the Gulf of Alaska—332.29 inches (838 cm). These are extremes. But there is no doubt that climate conditions dominate the way people live in Alaska.

In winter, they attach lamps or heaters to car engines. This is not to keep the water in radiators from freezing. It is to keep oil from congealing. Fire fighters put antifreeze in hydrants. Drivers know that parking meters do not work well when the temperature drops to $-20°$ F ($-29°$ C) and stop working after $-35°$ F ($-37°$ C). In Fairbanks, one of the coldest cities in the state, moisture freezes and causes an ice fog that lasts until the air warms up. Ice fogs often close the airport and automobile traffic slows to a few miles an hour.

All temperatures are affected by wind. A thermometer may register 10° F ($-12°$ C), but a 10-mile-an-hour (16-kph) wind will give a chill factor of $-9°$ F ($-22°$ C). This is tolerable. But a $-40°$ F ($-40°$ C) temperature with a 45-mile-an-hour (72-kph) wind will give a chill factor of −117° F (−82° C). Few people would be outside in this kind of weather. Even in less extreme conditions, most Alaskans stay indoors.

If they must go out, they cover all skin areas. Still, in this kind of weather, snow crystals are propelled with such force by the wind that they can go through seams in clothing. It is wise to walk backward to help breathing and to keep watery eyes from freezing eyelashes together. Even dogs must be protected in these extreme conditions. They wear caribou-hide moccasins, which are soft and pliable yet tough and insulated enough to keep their paws from freezing or being cut by ice.

Because of weather conditions, spring, summer, and fall are short. Another difference in the seasons is the varying daylight hours. In Barrow, between May 10 and August 2, the sun does not go below the horizon, causing continuous daylight. Between November 18 and January 24, the sun does not go above the horizon, causing continuous darkness. Farther south, Fairbanks has 21:49 hours of light on June 20 or 21 and only 3:42 hours of light on December 21 or 22. On those same days, Juneau has 18:18 hours of light and 6:21 hours of light.

During the winter, adults go to work and children go to school in the dark and return in the dark. Streetlights stay on all the time and mail carriers use flashlights to read addresses. When the temperature gets up to zero, some people have been known to bundle up and have a barbecue in their backyard!

During summer nights, people might be seen watering their flowers at two in the morning, putting foil over their windows to shut out the light at night, or playing baseball with no artificial lights. One of the highlights during the summer in Fairbanks is the Midnight Sun Baseball game, which begins at 11 P.M. on June 20 or 21. Some of the players who have taken part in Alaska's Baseball League are Bob Boon, Tom Seaver, and Dave Winfield.

Living in Alaska is difficult. Many try it but only a small percentage stay through the cycle of the seasons. Those who do earn the right to be called Alaskans.

11

ALASKA FACTS

Alaska is bounded on the east by Canada, on the north by the Arctic Ocean, on the west by the Arctic Ocean, Chukchi Sea, Bering Strait, and Bering Sea, and on the south by the Pacific Ocean and the Gulf of Alaska.

Alaska covers 586,412 square miles (938,260 sq km), which is one-fifth the area of the lower 48 states. If a map of Alaska were put over a map of the United States, it would cover the central part of the country from Canada south to Arkansas and from Indiana west to Colorado. Its southeastern corner would reach the Atlantic Ocean, and a portion of the Aleutian Islands would extend into the Pacific Ocean.

The population of Alaska is 521,000.

Alaska's territorial legislature gave women the right to vote in 1913, seven years before the 19th Amendment to the United States Constitution.

Point Barrow, Alaska, is the northernmost point in the United States.

Alaska has the easternmost and westernmost points in the country. This is because the 180th meridian, the dividing line between east and west longitudes, passes through the state.

Mount McKinley is the highest peak in North America.

Alaska's 33,904-mile (54,250-km) coastline, which includes islands, is longer than all the lower 48 states combined.

—68

Alaska has the world's largest concentration of bald eagles.
Alaska has no reptiles outside of captivity.

STATE SYMBOLS

In 1926, a 13-year-old seventh grade student named Benny Benson entered a flag design contest and won first prize. He was given a $1,000 scholarship, a watch, and the honor of having his design adopted in May 1927 as the flag of the territory of Alaska. Benny used the scholarship money to go to engineering school in Seattle. He returned to Alaska to work and died in Kodiak on July 2, 1972.

Flower: Blue forget-me-not

Tree: Sitka spruce

Bird: Willow ptarmigan

Fish: King salmon

Mineral: Gold

Gem: Jade

Motto: North to the Future

INDEX

DATE DUE